YOUR KNOWLEDGE HAS VALUE

Sarah Fuhrken

English Literature. Revision (Approaches)

Introduction to English Literature II (Universität Bremen)

GRIN Verlag

Bibliografische Information der Deutschen Nationalbibliothek:

Die Deutsche Bibliothek verzeichnet diese Publikation in der Deutschen National-
bibliografie; detaillierte bibliografische Daten sind im Internet über http://dnb.d-
nb.de/ abrufbar.

Imprint:

Copyright © 2014 GRIN Verlag GmbH
Druck und Bindung: Books on Demand GmbH, Norderstedt Germany
ISBN: 978-3-656-73403-1

This book at GRIN:

http://www.grin.com/en/e-book/279668/english-literature-revision-approaches

GRIN - Your knowledge has value

Der GRIN Verlag publiziert seit 1998 wissenschaftliche Arbeiten von Studenten, Hochschullehrern und anderen Akademikern als eBook und gedrucktes Buch. Die Verlagswebsite www.grin.com ist die ideale Plattform zur Veröffentlichung von Hausarbeiten, Abschlussarbeiten, wissenschaftlichen Aufsätzen, Dissertationen und Fachbüchern.

Visit us on the internet:

http://www.grin.com/

http://www.facebook.com/grincom

http://www.twitter.com/grin_com

Key Topics for Revision

1. Approaches and Methodologies in Literary Studies

<u>Key questions asked in Literary Theory:</u>
What is literature?
What constitutes a (literary/non-literary) text?
Are there different types of literature?
What's the relationship between literature and its environment?
What's the relationship between literature and other media?
What's the role of authors, text, readers?
How does form and content influence each other?
How is literature concerned with gender, politics, ethnicity etc?
Texts as products: In what kind of version has this text existed? (print, video etc)
Reproduction & reception: Who has been involved in making & responding?
Relations to the rest of the world: What are the various frames of reference & context
       within which the text was realized? What world-view does it represent?

<u>Typology of main theoretical approaches</u>

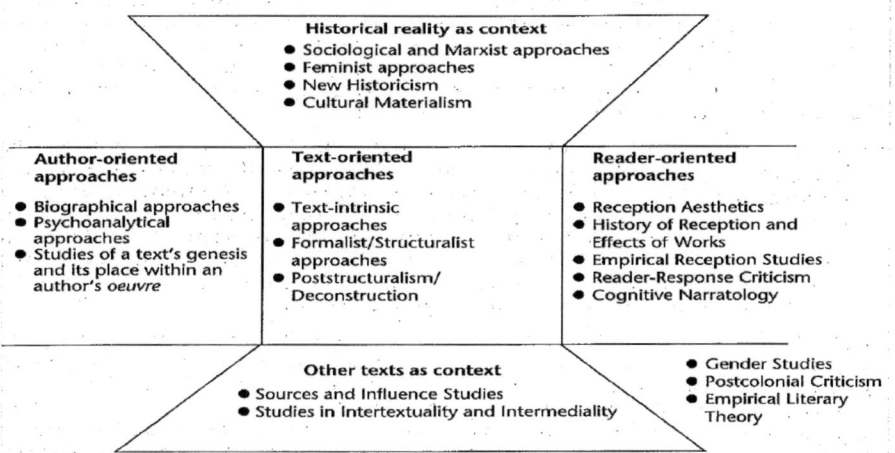

2. Words on the Page – Practical Criticism and (old) New Criticism

<u>Objectives and how to practice Practical Criticism and New Criticism:</u>
- requires close reading → text-centered

Practical Criticism: *I.A. Richards*
- no knowledge of the author (close-reading)
- ask people to comment freely on text → pick out intense/clichéd responses

New Criticism: *John Crowe Ransom*
- focus on text itself & rule out life of author and his intentions
- **Intentional Fallacy:** intention of author is not desirable/available for judging a work
- **Affective Fallacy:** confusion between poem and its results (what it is/what it does)

Wimsatt & Beardsley

- imagery, tension, contrast and balance are important in a good work
- aim of a poem: establish variety within unity
- look out for main tensions/contrasts, structuring of plot/argument, imagery...
- emphasise paradox, irony, unity →How are the parts related to the whole?

Main difference between the PC and NC:
- Practical criticism: commenting on a text freely
- New Criticism: commenting on a text with regard to certain aspects

Character and Characterisation:
3 meanings for character:
- distinctive nature & traits of a real person
- particular role played by a fictional figure
- a letter of the alphabet
- character can be a personal identity and a textual entity

characters can be described as
- rounded or flat
- individuals or types
- character-narrators or character-actors

characterisation: literary, linguistic & cultural means whereby a figure is constructed

3. Devices and Effects – Formalism into Functionalism

Major figures and objectives:
(Formalism turned into Functionalism)
Formalist Approach:
- text-centred, focus on features that make literature literary & poetry poetic
- devices that draw attention to language are **foregrounded**
- **background** is made up out of routine & ordinary language
- a work demonstrates its literariness when it:
  o defamiliarises habitual perceptions
  o foregrounds certain aspects & backgrounds others (with imagery etc.)
  o plays around with dimensions of time, space, narration

Functionalist Approach:
- socialised the abstract Formalist notions of defamiliarisation & foregrounding
- poetry disturbs & reforms routine language
- poetics is not restricted to poetry
- investigate:
  o aesthetic and social norms the text challenged/confirmed at the time
  o functions the text served & effects it had

Defamiliarisation and foregrounding:
Defamiliarisation:
- narrator overtly interrupts etc.
- catch attention of the reader
- unfamiliar things are interesting/striking
- realised through foregrounding

Foregrounding: *Mukarovsky & Havranek*
- 2 stages of foreground and background:
  - o foreground and background within the text
  - o foregrounding the text against the background outside the text
- what is familiar in one place/period might not be in another
- **deviation:** is a similar term but presupposes that ppl have same norms & values

Key terms: Heteroglossia:
heteroglossia: linguistic variety in literary work: another's speech in
          another's language
chronotope: expresses inseparability of space and time,   *Mikhail*
          defines genre & generic distinctions   *Bakhtin*
carnival: one set of cultural & aesthetic norms is overthrown by another

4. Mind and Person – Psychological Approaches

Major figures and models:
- we distinguish various selves from various others with words (I, you, my..)
- literature tells us about others inner lives & helps to explore own identities
- civilisation as result of human struggles to control animal drives & desires
- **unconscious:** we are not directly aware of it; includes our drives, forgotten & repressed childhood etc.
- **consciousness:** we <u>are</u> aware of it; includes perceptions, personal memories
- relation between the two is dynamic
- dreams are the "road to the unconscious"
- **latent content:** 3 ways in which meaning tends to be hidden:
  - o **condensation:** metaphors etc. → 2 or more meanings
  - o **displacement:** one item stands for another (ring for a special person)
  - o **symbolism:** one thing is identified with a certain function/meaning (ex: ring for wedding; heart for love etc.)
- **psychic instances:** *Sigmund Freud*
  - o **ego:** "I", part of self most concerned to gratify instinctual drives
  - o **id:** "other", the unconscious from which drives derive
  - o **super-ego:** "above-I", censor and judge, regulates the ego
- people's identities are never wholly their conscious view
- **Transactional analysis:** *Norman Holland:* transitional objects operate as potential space in which hopes & fears may be safely realised (ex: in a text)
- **Psychopolitics:** *Michel Foucault:* the personal is political, libido is subject to various economies (not as Freud implies only instinctual drive)

How to practise Psychological Approaches:
consider:
- What the text suggests about the **writer's** emotional, mental processes
- how you as a **reader** relate to & identify with the events, characters presented
- what the **language of the text** suggests about expression & repression
- auto/biography of the author: what are we not being told and why?
- aspects of the text that are under-represented

5. Reader-response theories and criticism / Hermeneutics

Word Play:
- play within and around language

- **poetry:** most complex form of word play
- **advertising:** word play is designed to make people pay
- **Levels of wordplay:**
    - **sound play:** sounds of a language become source of pleasure
    - **visual play:** uses letters, shapes, colors, fonts...
    - **lexical play:** single words are swapped around
    - **structural play:** (syntax) pleasurable tension

Writing & Reading, Response & Rewriting:
- **writing:** activity of making verbal marks on paper or other things
    - more permanent & finished than speech (uninterrupted)
    - detachable from place
    - reliant on punctuation & visual presentation
- **reading:** activity of engaging with those verbal marks
- **response:** forms of reaction & interaction
- **rewriting:** is writing & reading in some sense
- **re-creation:** all of these combined
- writing & reading as...
    - processes, products, attributes, verbs
    - occurs in print, handwriting, electronic modes
    - activities similar to but different from speaking & listening
- **Reception Theorists:** texts as part of a shifting relation with readers over time (*Hans Robert Jauss*)
- **implied reader:** intended by the author
- **blanks & vacancies:** filled by the actual readers   } *Wolfgang Iser*
- **affirmative negation:** through reading, the readers make sense of themselves not simply of the text
- **Reader-response Critics:** text analyses the reader and is seen as a site for projection of anxieties and hopes (*Norman Holland*)
- **readerly texts:** offer pleasure with a closed fictional world
- **writerly texts:** offer joy/ecstasy of participation in construction of a fictional world   } *Roland Barthes*
- the readers also control how far a text is readerly/writerly
- **kinds of response:**
    - **passive or submissive reading:** reading "with the grain", accepting perceived versions of reality
    - **oppositional or counter-reading:** reading "against the grain", oppose the text's meanings
    - **alternative or negotiated reading:** neither "with" nor "against the grain"

6. Class and Community – Marxism, Cultural Materialism and New Histoicism

Major figures and concepts:
- concerned with social/political aspects of interpretation & understanding texts in social & historical context
- language is grasped for what it <u>does</u>, not what it <u>is</u>
- attention to:
    - modes of production (technologies & social relations)
    - relations between economic base & ideological superstructure
    - power-relations

Key concepts of New Historicism *(Stephen Greenblatt & Louis Montrose)*
- a Marxist approach
- American counterpart of **Cultural Materialism**
- socially sensitive but less politically than Cultural Materialism
- recognise power relations in a text's moment of production & reproduction

Dynamic model of ideology: *(Raymond Williams)*
- culture as the whole way of living of a people
- **dominant:** aspects of the text that represent central ways of seeing → present
- **residual:** once central but now superseded ways of seeing → past
- **emergent:** maybe new ways of seeing, still in progress → future
- every text can be grasped as a site where discourses of past, present & future meet; refracting ideologies as part of a continuing process & site of stuggle

7. Gender and Sexuality – Feminism, Masculinity and Queer Theory

Key concerns of Gender Studies/changing concepts of gender
- concerned with nature and representation of women and men
- **sex:** refers to biological differences
- **gender:** culturally constructed, social make-up, dynamic
- we are born male/female but we learn to be feminine/masculine
- **stereotypes:** don't apply to all wo/men or to all historical periods & cultures
- **sexuality:** refers to sexual orientation
- *Michel Foucault:* foundation to understanding of **homosocial/homophobic**

Major figures and concepts:
- **Feminism:** challenge traditional power of men, politically motivated
- **Anglo-American & Australian approach** *(Lakoff):* more practical & overtly political; overthrow man-centred language
- **French approach:** *(Kristeva):* more theoretical; psychoanalytic
- **Black, ethnic, postcolonial:** *(Spivak):* political & psychological
- **Gay and lesbian writers:** *(Butter):* what it is like to be queer
- first: emphasis on images & representations of women by male writers
- man were attacked for making women "sex objects"
- then: more emphasis on women's struggle to represent themselves
consider:
- sexual composition & orientation of your course & how evident these are in the texts that you read
- kinds of women and men represented in the text
  - tension between/among the sexes?
  - what is not represented?
  - how do the characters act inside and outside the home
  - gendered ways of speaking, acting, dressing...
  - sex, sexual orientation and gender of the writer
  - gender roles and sexual practices at that time

8. Relativities – Poststructuralism and Postmodernism

Major figures and concepts:
- see texts as shifting relations & ongoing projects
- both are related contemporary movements; celebrate difference/openness

Poststructuralism (*Barthes, Derrida, Foucault*)
- out of academic milieu (Linguistics, Philosophy, Anthropology)
- concerned with language
- **Structuralism** (sign system finished, with centre, whole systems, sense-making)
- sign system as incomplete, unfinished fragment with many potential centres or none at all
- holes in systems, nonsense-making
- deconstruction, absences, gaps, silences

Postmodernism:
- out of artistic and literary milieu
- concerned with global communications
- **Modernism:** non-realist representation, stream of consciousness, multiple points of view, fragmentary techniques
- multimedia (advertising, popular music etc.), multiple viewpoint, intertextuality
- **sign systems** (*Saussure*):
  - concept of sign is fundamental
  - understanding of communication
  - **parole:** utterance of a word
  - **langue:** language system as a whole
- **model of culture** (*Lévi-Strauss*):
  - all things have symbolic function (goods for thinking)
- **deconstruction** (*Foucault*):
  - focus to texts in context as intertextual constructs
  - many fragments of history don't add up as a whole
  - **discontinuity** is important
- **condition** (*Lyotard*):
  - everybody plays a role with all their energy
  - one can insist that another game be played
  - one is not to believe that theirs is the only game
- attention to:
  - differences
  - centres & margins
  - closed & open structures
  - narratives

Intertextuality:
- relation between two texts
- **explicit intertextuality:** overtly; easy to prove
- **implicit intertextuality:** indirect; harder to prove
- **inferred intertextuality:** text that reader take to understand the text; most open

9. Ethnicities – Postcolonialism and Multiculturalism

Major figures and concepts:
- concerned with effects of colonialism, experiencing life in multicultural world
- most English-speaking countries are multicultural
- colonies had a lot of impact on language
- **colonisation:** activity of making colonies
- **colonialism:** system of having colonies
- **slave trade triangle:** GB→Africa→ America→GB
- **postcolonialism:** state of those countries that achieved independence
- **multiculturalism:** awareness of the plural & hybrid nature of all cultures

Consider:
- Where in the world are you? –does your family come from? When? Why?
- How far do you identify with coloniser/colonised?
- What ethnic or cultural groups come in contact with you?
- language you use, literature that you study
- What varieties of English do you use/prefer?
- Where in the world did the text come from?
- Is it **ethnocentric**? (negative; centres one culture)
- Are racial/ethnic stereotypes challenged?
- **Neocolonialism:** exercise of international power through economic & commercial rather than military means

Key terms: Standards and Standardisation, Varieties and Variation
- Is there a standard English? How did it become standard?
- **Standard:**
  - average, routine, common
  - prescribed measure of quantity/quality
- **Varieties:** linguistic products of difference
- **Variation:** historical processes of differentiation
- a standard is itself a variety subject to continuing variation

10. The New Electicism? Ethics, Aesthetics, Ecology

Ethics, Aesthetics, Ecology:
- **Electicism:** activity of gathering, selecting, adapting different models
- **Ethics:** attention to matters of right and wrong
  - concerned with justice, right & responsibility
  - good or bad ethically → morally, politically
  - awareness of impact when using certain words (loaded language)
  - drafting of official documents
  - speech acts: it has serious, life-changing consequences
  - words are tools or weapons
- **Aesthetics:** idea of the beautiful
  - concerned with wholeness, satisfaction etc.
  - good or bad aesthetically → formally, perceptually
- **Ecology:** study interrelations in natural systems (who process on to other systems)
- Ethics, Aesthetics & Ecology are concerned with wholeness & universality; recognition that values differ and vary

Re-evaluations and Re-presentations of people in place and time
Household, family, community
- based on property, rank, blood ties, friendship?
- with or without animals and servants?
- Is there a sense of home?
Identity and Identification: roots or routes:
- Is there a sense of homelessness? – Migrants, Nomads
Life and death, time and change:
- How are the cycles of birth, life, death realised?
- Are fundamental activities like eating, drinking, sleeping, sex realised?
People a part of or apart from nature:
- **versions of pastoral:** country-dwellers represented in idyllically, idealised simplicity
- **city as second nature:** delights and distresses of urban living

- **science fiction: Utopias and Dystopias**
  - **Utopia:** imaginary ideal place
  - **Dystopia:** imaginary horrible place

Local and global:
- How far is the text conceived in local or global terms?

Nation states and international relations:
- national or international dimension to the text

11. From Literary to Media Studies

Inter-Art Studies/Intermediality
- **Music and Literature:** literature in music, references to music in literature, combinations of music and literature
- **Art and Literature:** descriptions of images play significant role in contemporary lit.
- **Photography and Literature:** photographs give impression of immediate reality
- **Mediality:** perceived reality influenced through media
- **Intermediality:** study of interrelations between different media
- **intermedial:** crossing of borders between media
- **intramedial:** only one medium, reference to sth of the same medium (2 films)
- **transmedia:** certain style etc. across variety of media

New Media Genres:
- Analysis of film & TV:
  - examination of production conditions
  - investigation of technical developments
  - image, sound, story and narrative mode
  - distance between camera and its object; angle, speed
- camera as omniscient narrator
- voice-over represents consciousness
- **deceleration:** slow motion
- **acceleration:** fast motion